ISBN-13: 978-1518610905

ISBN-10: 1518610900

DEDICATION

To my mother, Virginia Walker, who told me many things when I was a young girl, still in elementary and high school. She told me things she thought would prepare me for life as a woman, a black woman, in America:

"You have to be better than other people to get ahead in this world."

"You have to learn how to get along with all kinds of people to succeed."

And, her trademark line, "You have to suffer to be beautiful."

That last pronouncement usually was said while someone was combing my coarse, curly, knotty hair before I grew up and began regularly straightening it with chemicals and heat.

My mother was a wonderful, kind and gentle woman, and even though this advice might seem harsh, she meant it in the best possible way. She would be happy to hear this:

Mommy, I refuse to suffer any longer. And I'm still beautiful.

CONTENTS

Acknowledgements

Foreword

Cover illustration by artist Ebony Iman Dallas

Photo gallery by Valerie Rollins Vaughn of Withunmind Photography

Ebony Iman Dallas photos by Jaleecia Ates Photography

Other photos provided by the authors.

TO KAREN AND ASHLIE

ACKNOWLEDGMENTS

Thanks to the women and men who graciously gave of their time and talents to produce the wonderful essays you are about to read. They have a lot to say, and I appreciate the work they put into these chapters.

Thanks to my copy editor, B.G. We all need an editor.

By Yvette Walker

My sister will tell you that I shocked the heck out of her and the rest of my family when I announced that I would wean my hair of chemical relaxer and go natural in November 2012.

My sister and niece had gone natural years before, growing their hair into dreadlocks. My sister's were thinner, "cultivated," and my niece's locs were chunkier. Both played with hair color.

I wouldn't have expected this of myself either – I loved the "creamy crack," a substance that made my hair easy to manage.

It cost. Both in money and in the health of my hair.

I needed to return to the salon every 2-3 weeks and get an extra application of relaxer cream every 6 weeks, exactly. Each application cost $100, which included a cut.

Relaxer – whether it contains lye or not – breaks down the hair shaft and goes into the cuticle, making it lie down, which gives the appearance of smoother, straighter hair.

And it lasts, especially in colder climes. In hot, damp weather there is a tendency for the hair to revert or to "go back." That would mean another trip to the salon.

There was a reason I went natural, and it didn't have to do with ethnicity.

From my observations, most African American women jump into the natural hair experience out of fear, fun or frustration: fear of damage done to hair after years of using chemicals; fun, for a change of pace; frustration of the amount of time and money needed to consistently maintain relaxed hair.

No matter which, most don't have the information they need at the start of their natural hair journey.

I am a middle-aged African American woman and have relaxed my hair for more than half my life. How could I manage my hair any less than bone straight?

Could I learn to deal with my hair, and more importantly, could I learn to style it for work and for school?

My trigger was fear. After years of using relaxer and color, my stylist gave me a choice: either ditch the color or the relaxer.

The choice was easy. Color all the way. I have grey hair, and I have had it since I was in my 20s. My mother greyed early, too. I get it from her. Now, my mother was a silver fox. Her hair came in beautiful vertical streaks that looked like she did it on purpose.

Half my hair is patchy grey and I'm NOT ready to acquiesce!

Shortly after my mother died, I decided to let is all go grey. As an homage to her memory. Months passed and the grey hair grew out, replacing the bottle-colored dark strands. More than half my hair in the front was silver.

My friends praised my hair, how it was so shiny and silver. One night at a Christmas party, a co-worker's husband decided to pay me a compliment. "It's pretty. You look just like Della Reese."

Della Reese is an actress thirty years my senior. I was 40 at the time and did NOT find that a compliment.

I was not amused. And I dyed my hair the very next week.

So, you see, the answer was easy. The relaxer had to go.

The women in my family have thick, long coarse hair. That's a blessing and a curse: a blessing from the point of view of women who have thinning hair; a curse from the point of view of my comb and my tender scalp.

When I was a girl, my mother sent me to my best friend's mother for the every other week press-and-curl. This was a ritual where she would wash my hair, comb it out, dry it under a bonnet dryer, apply hair grease and then straighten it with heat.

Here, "Heat" means a metal comb and a gas stove burner. The "hot comb" was a multi-sensory experience: the heat of the fire burning your skin, the sound of the grease sizzling as the hot comb moved down from scalp to end, and the smell of the hair singeing.

Oh, yes, there was burning of hair every time. Even the most experienced women – be it professional beautician or home kitchen stylist – burned hair and skin during a hot comb procedure. Maybe just a little, maybe a lot.

The burn made you jump, and that caused the hot comb to jump and maybe burn you again. It certainly vexed the wielder of the comb, who would tongue lash you with the words, "Sit still, little girl!"

Girls endured the hot comb until chemical relaxers became mainstream and were sold on drugstore shelves. Relaxers were developed in the early 1900s but it wasn't until the late 1970s did you begin to see easily accessible home perm kits.

I got a relaxer at a salon when I was a sophomore in high school. All through high school I wore a "Farrah Fawcett" and in college I got bangs with long sides. When I graduated, it became a side part with fringy upturned ends, and later, side-swept bangs.

I traveled the country as a newspaper journalist and my hair put my best face forward. For a time, natural hair might have been a hindrance, but no longer. Not in my profession. My colleagues on TV have their own hairs to bear, as professional standards are different for broadcast than for print or radio.

I loved my swingy, bouncin' and behavin' hair. I loved it for decades, but I had to let it go. My hair had become damaged and something had to be done.

That something was going natural. And here I am today. I have learned that looking professional with natural is not an oxymoron. There are myriad styles a woman can rock in the classroom, in the workplace and even in the board room.

Yes, I've heard the stories. The woman whose boss told her to take the day off when she came in with a big Afro.

The intern whose new employer told him to cut off his dreadlocks if he wanted to complete the internship (you'll read more about that later.)

I wear my hair loose in ringlets. I twist it into updos. I pull it back into a loose, messy bun. And yes, occasionally, I even have it straightened with a hot blow dryer and a flat iron.

A woman can achieve a winning style in a business setting. If that's your fear, you can let that go. Natural hair needn't make you a loser at work.

It only takes your self-confidence and a put-together office ensemble to make it work.

Many others have come to the same conclusion. The journey may be different but we've all passed the finish line.

We've passed go. We've collected 200 curly coils. We won.

CHAPTER 1

GLOBAL DARK AND LOVELY

by Alison Bethel McKenzie

H er name is Amber. And she is beautiful. Some people think she is beautiful because her hair is long, straight and natural. It falls near her waist. Or, at least, it used to.

This Bahamian beauty has recently decided to cut her hair and lock it. That means she has chosen dreadlocks. And, oh, what a stir it has made.

"Even I look on TV nowadays and all the girls and women have lightened skin and it has to be blemish-free and straight, straight hair," says Amber in a delicate Bahamian accent, before surmising, "Hair has no value."

Does it define how beautiful you are? I ask. "No.

"I used to get hate when my hair was long and now [that I have dreadlocks] I get hate. You can't please people. They used to be jealous of my long hair … I used to get hate when I had long, long hair. … They used to come. 'That real?' Yeah. It real. I used to open up my hair and let them feel my hair.

"When people see my locs now, they like 'Where all your hair gone?'

If you walk on the street now, 9 in 10 women are not wearing their natural hair. When I locked my hair, it was like me saying, I am more than my hair," she told me.

Says her male cousin, "They still have that self-hate within them."

On the other hand, I am a woman who is proud of being so-called "dark and lovely," a spin on the permanent hair straightening process that I use so regularly.

I am a hair whore.

I go to the hairdresser every week without fail. I deep condition and straighten and, on occasion, flat iron. While I don't frown on the "Happy to Be Nappy Movement," I also embrace choice. Straight. Curly. Wavy. Permed. Locked. Twists. Wigs. And, kinda – weave.

I am no less black, or pro-black because I choose straightened hair.

My girlfriend in Austria is a formal model and her hair of choice is weave. She likes it long and she likes it straight. She just doesn't get why anyone would choose otherwise and often comments on how unkempt the modern afro looks.

She is not alone. Many of my acquaintances in Ghana, where I lived for just over a year, feel the same way. Nearly every middle-class woman I encountered in Accra had hair extensions or weave.

It made them feel more modern, more beautiful – some would say, less African. I was amazed at their dedication to straight, fake hair. It made me sad.

I have traveled the world and have lived on three continents. No matter where I go, the fascination with hair is very real.

For black women all over the world it carries a political and social message – whether it is the message of assimilation or of revolution.

It is why the hair straightening and hair weave industries are so wealthy and growing at an amazing rate.

Black women learn to focus on their hair at a young age. When I was growing up in South Florida my sisters and I would go to the hairdresser every Friday to have our hair pressed and curled. The resulting smooth and flowing hair gave us an immediate, and albeit false, sense of empowerment. Sad, but true. And we loved it.

"Hair can give you a false sense of power," says Amber. "You are a hair idol."

Motivating this obsession with hair is the media – and men.

It is no secret that men covet long hair. Even the Bible notes that hair is a woman's crown and glory.

But for me and others, it has to be more than that. My hair is an extension of me and how I feel on any given day. I wear it straight, I braid it, I wrap it in scarves.

It is about looking in the mirror and being able to say, "I am beautiful no matter what crown I wear today."

And I am no less black or no less pro-black because of my choice.

Alison Bethel McKenzie has more than 30 years of experience as an award-winning reporter, bureau chief, senior editor and media trainer. From 1995-2000, she was deputy business editor and then senior assistant city editor at The Boston Globe. In 2000, she joined The Detroit News as features editor, then served as the paper's Washington, D.C. bureau chief from 2001-2006. She joined the Legal Times in Washington, D.C. in 2006 as executive editor, and later the Nassau Guardian in The Bahamas as managing director.

She spent a year in Accra, Ghana, for the Washington, D.C.-based International Center for Journalists, as a Knight International Journalism Fellow. In August 2009, she joined the International Press Institute based in Vienna, Austria, as deputy director before becoming the institute's Executive Director a year later. She is the first woman and the first person of color in IPI's 64-year history to hold the position. She sits on the board of directors of Al Jazeera America and is a member and former board member of the National Press Club in Washington, D.C. Bethel is a native of Miami, Fla.

CHAPTER 2

CANCER & A BOTTLE OF CARE FREE CURL

by Angela Tuck

My natural hair journey started somewhat unceremoniously in a rainy hospital parking lot with a pair of dollar store scissors.

My dear father had just been diagnosed with Stage 4 lung cancer and our entire family was devastated. My then 78-year-old father had never smoked and aside from a broken ankle he suffered while playing baseball, he'd never been hospitalized. Now comes this cancer monster. Upon hearing the diagnosis, Daddy looked the doctor in the eye and told him he was not afraid of cancer. His faith was his sword and shield. If God never did another thing for him, he'd already done enough.

The rest of us went into full attack mode, questioning the doctors and researching this beast called non-small cell lung cancer. I was a ball of emotion and in the midst of it all, the pollen was causing my skin and scalp allergies to flare up in a big way.

An oozing scalp infection matted my hair on the left side. My dermatologist called in a familiar prescription and I headed to the dollar store on a mission to get a pair of scissors and some product. Yep, I started this natural hair walk with a $3 bottle of Soft Sheen Carson's Care Free Curl; the one in the bright yellow bottle with the bold red letters.

Somehow, cutting the perm out of my hair seemed the natural answer to soothing the pain of my father's diagnosis. And it would let my stinging scalp breathe. So I stood in the parking lot of my father's hospital and let the rain saturate my hair. Then, using the mirror on my car visor, I did what I had seen my hairdresser do for years. I extended the roughly five inches of hair in my on my head with my fingers and began cutting those straight, pointy permed ends.

I used the plastic dollar store bag to catch my wet hair then tossed it into the trash on my way into the hospital. Once inside, I decided to visit the hospital bathroom to get a better view of my do-it-myself haircut. Not bad I thought, as I applied some of the Care Free Curl to the two inches of hair I had left on my head. At that moment, my hair was the least of my concerns. I had whacked it off in a matter of five minutes with not a second thought about what would come next.

What came next is tricky. As soon as I entered my father's hospital room, he asked me "What did you do to your hair?" My father is a traditionalist who is not a big fan of change – or natural hair. He is used to the daughter who perms her hair every eight weeks and keeps her sassy short cut styled to perfection with once-weekly hair appointments.

Ditto for my husband, oldest daughter and nine-year-old grandson. They all took one look at my natural hair and asked simply, "Why?"

"Because I could," was my reply. No matter what others think of my natural, tight curls, I like them. The style is simple, sassy and gives me a freedom that I desperately need at this time in my life. Put simply, this works for me and has given me an unexpected burst of self-confidence.

I do reserve the right to revert back to the creamy crack at some point. But for now, bring on the natural hair products (I've tried six or seven other brands since ditching the Care Free Curl). The choice is mine and mine alone.

Angela Tuck is the owner of Angela Tuck & Associates, an Atlanta-based writing, editing and training firm. She is an award-winning writer and editor who has worked for the Atlanta Journal-Constitution, the Tampa Bay Times, the Detroit Free Press and the Lexington, Ky. Herald-Leader.

Her blog, lovemypeople.me, contains her musings about faith, family and culture. She and her husband Joe have two daughters and are the proud grandparents of Austin and Olivia. Contact Angela at angeladtuck@gmail.com.

CHAPTER 3

THE KITCHEN

by Linda Jones

I f you can't stand the heat, stay out of the kitchen.

In 2008, during the Democratic bid for president, the famous words of former President Harry Truman were echoed by former first Lady Hillary Clinton.

She invoked the quote in Iowa when she was taking heat from her male rivals just before the January caucuses. She repeated it a second time, when she faced her remaining opponent Senator Barack Obama, adding a sassy tag line.

"... Just speaking for myself," Hillary said, "I am very comfortable in the kitchen."

Right then I knew that Hillary was not an Adult Survivor of the Hot Comb. If she was, she would NEVER have cited the kitchen as a place of comfort. For Adult Survivors of the Hot Comb— ASH for short, the kitchen was a place of dread.

ASHy women are Black women who lived to tell about having

their kinky hair straightened with steel tooth combs that were placed in fire. Those traumatic and horrid grooming rituals took place in the kitchen.

When Hillary spoke of her "comfort" in the kitchen during her campaign remarks, no doubt she was referring to the room that the general public knows as the place where food is cooked. But Adult Survivors of the Hot Comb know all too tragically well that the kitchen is also the place where our *hair* was cooked.

I am a recovering ASH. I still shudder whenever I think about those Saturday nights when my sisters and I sat in that sweltering kitchen, unwillingly waiting until it was our turn to get our rebellious hair pressed, or – to be more precise – o-pressed. That steel-toothed hot comb was my mother's weapon of nap destruction.

In our household, the smell of burning hair by hot comb was as common as the smell of fried chicken.

The way the comb was heated depended on what kind of stove we had. When we had a gas stove, the comb was placed over a low flame. When my father bought a more modern electric stove, the comb was placed on the red hot spiral burner.

When the comb got smoking hot, my mother removed it from the heat, waved it in the air a few times and blew on it, as if her breath would cool it off.

It did not. The comb was still hot and my hair still sizzled when it connected. I ducked and dodged, but I could not escape until all traces of my nappy hair texture was gone and my hair was "done" — at least temporarily. All it took for my hair to revert right back home to its natural state was any form of precipitation – water, sweat, steam, mist, morning dew. When our hair snapped back, we were taken back to the kitchen and the ritual started all over again.

As strange as it may sound, as much as I dreaded the kitchen hair-straightening sessions, all ASHy women knew that our mothers' actions were not intended to be abusive. In their minds they were performing acts of love.

Our mothers wanted our hair to be pretty, and they were conditioned to believe that pretty image did not include having nappy textured hair.

So as a result, we had to sit in the kitchen and take the heat. And contrary to Hillary's reference, we were not comfortable. This is no criticism of Hillary's rhetorical claim that the kitchen is her comfort zone. It is just my humble observation that kitchen comfort is definitely in the mind- – and on the head – of the beholder.

The kitchen has still another cultural connotation for people with nappy hair.

The kitchen is also the nickname for the hair that resides at the nape of our necks. It is the place where our most rebellious kinks congregate. Hair that takes root and grows in our kitchens is the nappiest, curliest, kinkiest and the most resistant to change.

We already know that in unenlightened circles, nappiness is viewed as an unacceptable hair texture and the word "nappy" is a pejorative term. In that context, you can imagine how much our nappy kitchens are viewed with disdain. Those of us who are deeply afflicted with nap denial have gone through great lengths to obliterate that shameful section of our heads. If it took a double dose of chemicals or removal by razor to keep our kitchens in the closet, it was worth it.

But negative perceptions notwithstanding, the kitchen was a powerful place.

It was the area that my mother struggled with most during my hot comb rite of passage. While the hair on the rest of my head readily surrendered to the smoking hot comb, my kitchen did not give up without a fight.

I have a name of honor for my kitchen hair. I call it "Nap Turner." My Nap Turner hair reminds me of the heroic slave Nat Turner who rebelled against oppression. "Nap Turner," my nappy "hairo," righteously rebels against being o-pressed by hot combs and chemical relaxers.

Even the nap-savvy Afro pick has lost a few teeth during expeditions into our kitchens. And pity our love partners of another hue who expected smooth sailing when they tried to run their fingers through our hair. When they passionately navigated their way into the density of our kitchens they were unexpectedly thrown off "coarse." Much like disappearing into the void of the Bermuda Triangle, those probing fingers got forever lost in the kitchen kink!

Our kitchens have been such a deeply rooted institution that they have even commanded the respect of the Ivy League. Henry Louis Gates Jr., the esteemed Harvard professor, paid homage in his memoir, "Colored People."

"If there was ever one part of our African past that resisted assimilation, it was the kitchen," Brother Gates proclaims. "No matter how hot the iron, no matter how powerful the chemical, no matter how stringent the mashed-potatoes-and-lye formula of a man's "process," neither God nor woman nor Sammy Davis Jr., could straighten the kitchen.

The kitchen was permanent, irredeemable, invincible kink. Unassimilably African. No matter what you did, no matter how hard you tried, nothing could de-kink a person's kitchen."

How's that for validation?

Linda Jones is a stylist of words and uses hairstyle as a device to raise awareness about Black lifestyle and culture. She is the founder of A Nappy Hair Affair and originator of the grass-roots hair grooming sessions known as Hair Days. One of her supporters dubbed her "Mosetta" (as in female Moses), for fostering a feeling of freedom from hair bondage and negative self-perceptions.

Linda is author of *"Nappyisms: Affirmations for Nappy-Headed People and Wannabes!"* An essay from her book is featured in Chicken Soup for the African American Woman's Soul and in "Tenderheaded: A Comb Bending Collection of Hair Stories." A freelance writing consultant, Linda runs ManeLock Communications, a professional writing service. Through her lively 'hairepy' sessions Linda promotes nappiness, self-appreciation and self-pride.

CHAPTER 4

GODDESS HAIR

by Telesa Hines

My hair is so much bigger than me
Because no one wants to be the one who has to
sit behind me in a crowded movie theatre
Because women with hair like mine
Could be the first to win Olympic gold medals
And set records for not just Black America
For all of America
Instead of applauding them for making history
Not Black history
American History
My hair will be the trending topic
Women with hair like mine are told
Tone it down, straighten it out, relax
If I choose to just be
In the hair God gave me
I'm a rebel
A troublemaker
A pot stirrer
I am expected to punish my tresses

With harmful chemicals and brutal heat
Just for showcasing any evidence my African heritage
I'm expected to wear someone else's hair
From India, Brazil or Malaysia
The more African my hair is, the worse it is, the nappier it is
Women who look just like me
Turn their noses up and curl their lips
In looks of disgust
And say,
"She needs to do something with that hair!"
The more European my hair is, the better it is
When my curls are loose and manageable
Or nonexistent
Women who look just like me
Smile and touch it, with longing twinkling in their eyes
And say things like, "You got that good hair."
UnGodly hair is coveted hair
Good hair is the furthest thing from Black hair
Black hair is bad hair
My hair is bigger than me because
It has prevented generations of women who look like me
from learning to swim
Or singing in the rain
Or making snow angels
My hair is bigger than me
Because women who look like me
Women with hair like mine
Have been conditioned to believe
That God's own personal creation
Is somehow not good enough
How dare I
Look my creator in the eye

And say this hair is bad
This hair is nappy
My hair is bigger than me because God gave it to me
This hair is Godly
Tied to a collective unconscious of sovereign blood
God gave me this hair that defies the laws of gravity
God gave me this hair that grows up
Instead of down
Chasing the sun
God gave me this hair that's strong enough to support a crown
God gave me this hair with its dominant Eve genes
With its 9-ether chemical composite
Melanin absorbing
Having an intimate love affair with the Sun
Possessing the love, strength and devotion of Auset
God made these curls
How can they be too tight?
God made these coils
How can they be too kinky?
God gave me this 'Fro
How can it be too big?
This is God's hair
This is Goddess hair

Telesa Hines is a native of Gulfport, Mississippi and has been writing since she was old enough to read. As an Army brat, she grew up mostly in Germany and was blessed with the opportunity to travel the world. Telesa not only writes poetry, but also short stories, novels, songs and plays. Currently, she has a blog called "Reality TH" where she is candid about her battles with losing weight, her misadventures with love and dating, financial woes that come along with being an up and coming artist, and her everyday life.

She is the proud single mother of two amazing boys and hopes that seeing her grind and hustle hard for her dreams will show them that they can do anything they put their mind to. Telesa recently stepped out on faith again, and relocated to Atlanta to pursue a career as a professional actress. She hopes to be in position to give other up-and-coming artists the same opportunities that have been afforded to her. And above all, her mission is to always glorify her creator in all that she does.

CHAPTER 5

NEVER DREAD CHANGE

by Ebony Iman Dallas

"OUCH!" I yelled, "Momma, you're pullin' too hard!"

POP! She slapped the back of my head with a 5-inch-by-5-inch comb with the words "The Afro Master" printed across the top. This was a throwback from Mom's natural hair days.

"Shut up and stop pulling away. You are gonna be late for school!"

She gripped me tighter between her legs as I sat on the floor. I hated this routine. I am very tender-headed, and stress associated with getting my hair combed marked the beginning of each day for me.

My sister and I had very thick, long hair that we were not allowed to cut the first 15 years of our life. I chose to get rid of mine immediately, cutting my hair into a "mushroom," with the top half reaching the bottom of my ear and the back hugging my shoulder blades.

Hair brought lots of undesired attention for me. Sneers, and sideways, "you've got that good hair" comments followed by a slight rolling of the eyes didn't really leave me feeling all that good about it.

Not always unpleasant encounters, but often. So following my 15th birthday, I decided to get rid of as much as possible.

Following the mushroom was a T-Boz, from the musical group TLC – a replica with the back tapering my neck and as it circled around to the front of my face, gradually reaching my shoulders.

Around age 6, I received the kiddie starter perm kit, Just for Me. The little bottle of extra conditioner in the box smelled like candy — an extra treat, not to mention the tearless daily hair sessions.

In 2000, my sophomore year at University of Central Oklahoma, I decided to go natural. Not such a popular thing at the time, but it made sense to me.

I straightened my hair far less than in years prior, and wore it curly half the time. When I wanted to straighten it, I'd just press it out.

So I cut my permed hair, leaving about four inches at the longest point, and allowed it to grow out. This went on for about four years before a trip to Nairobi, Kenya, where every hair salon my aunt Muna and I visited featured a cast of Caucasian women modeling their hair on the walls.

These were the promoted images of beauty, which looked nothing like the beautiful women in each stall waiting to give or receive a "blow out."

It was then that I decided to never straighten my hair again.

Never again. Well, that almost lasted. To this day I wear my hair in its natural curly state far more than straight, but I'm not a Nazi about it. I do what I want.

My 35th birthday is only a few days away from the moment I am typing these words. To mark my journey and some pretty major life transitions, I've decided to lock my hair. Allowing my hair to go through this process is a reminder to enjoy the journey.

Remember, it's not meant to be perfect and only gets better with time. So I'm like a 35-year-old bottle of fine wine.

Cheers.

Ebony
Dallas,
before.

Ebony
Dallas,
after
loc'ing
her hair.

Photos by
Jaleecia
Ates

Ebony Iman Dallas is a painter, designer and founder of Afrikanation Artists Organization.

She received her BA Journalism/Art degree from the University of Central Oklahoma and an MFA in Design from California College of the Arts in San Francisco. She is currently a Creative Designer at The Oklahoman Media Company.

Through her artwork, she combines rich and fiery hues with whimsical forms in order to bring the spirit and energy of her subjects to life.

With a focus on authenticity and progress, her artwork takes form organically, with each line determining the shape and direction of the next.

CHAPTER 6

HAIRGATE 2006:
THE DREAD SCANDAL!

by Mashaun D. Simon

S NIPP!

It was the haircut heard around the nation – about three weeks after the fact actually.

When word spread that Black Enterprise, the black-owned business magazine for which I spent my summer interning requested I cut off a year's worth of growth in the form of locs, and I obliged, EVERYONE was outraged.

SNIPP!

Yes, I admit it; I am guilty.

Yes, you got me; I am the one who did it.

Put the cuffs on me, lock me up and throw away the key.

I.

Cut.

My.

Hair.

Now that we have the introductions out of the way, stop gawking at me; close your mouths.

Stop judging me.

SNIPP!

Funny isn't it?

Not so much actually.

It was a situation that, for all intents and purposes, took over my life and much of my summer that year.

Here I was, at the precipice of my young career, working and living in New York City.

Here I was … being told to assimilate, to cut my hair, to oblige by the "dress code," to choose my career over my image …

SNIPP!

Looking back at that time in my young life, I made a decision I thought was best.

I had no interest in being a poster child for their movement.

Yet everyone else was outraged.

SNIPP!

"You could have worked anywhere this summer and able to keep your hair."

Maybe.

SNIPP!

"It's about principle."

Yeah, I hear you.

SNIPP!

"Your civil rights were violated!"

Oh really?!

SNIPP!
SNIPP!
SNIPP!

I do not regret the decision.

Hair, stereotypically, is a big deal within the black community. I get it.

Expression, cultural commodification, and identity are at the root of such issues regarding hair.

But looking back on that moment, the experience of growing out my hair again, re-loc'ing and cutting them again in my final year of seminary, it all comes down – for me – to individual freedom.

What frustrates me about the black community is this argument that we all have to believe a certain way, see the world a certain way, share the same perspectives, and be riled about the same issues in the same way.

I do not agree.

At the same time, I also believe we all should be free to express ourselves in the way we see fit, as long as it does not impact the lives, beliefs and perceptions of others in damaging ways.

I also realize we all are not there – and this society as a whole has a long way to go before individualism and collective individualism becomes a respected reality.

We all have our role to play.

We all have our work to do.

We all have our place in history.

BY cutting my hair, I did not lose any part of my individuality.

I did not lose any of my life force, or become weaker.

At the end of the day, it was a choice I made for my well-being.

As India.Arie put it, "I am not my hair!"

She's right!

Now, who wants cake?!

Mashaun D. Simon is a minister and award-winning writer based in Atlanta whose writing focuses on issues of race, sexuality, identity and faith. A native of Atlanta, Simon started his professional career as a print journalist in 1999 as an intern at the historic Atlanta Daily World newspaper. Simon joined the staff of the Atlanta Journal Constitution as a Breaking News reporter in 2009. For a year he served on the staff of the digital department of the AJC while also discerning a call to ministry. By the summer of 2010, Simon would end his working relationship with the AJC and enroll in the Master of Divinity program at the Candler School of Theology, Emory University. While obtaining his degree, Simon worked for the Communications Department of Candler while also contributing to TheGrio.com where he focused many of his interests on black religiosity and sexuality. He graduated in the spring of 2013.

Simon's byline has also been seen in *Black Enterprise* magazine, *BlackEnterprise.com*, *QSR Magazine*, *Southern Voice*, *Written Magazine* and Bloomberg News, *The Island Packet,* and *Essence Magazine.*

He now serves on the leadership team of House of Mercy Everlasting Church (HOME) in College Park, GA.

CHAPTER 7

SUBMISSION

by Holly Lynn Wise

Hair had always been part of my costume.

As a prop in the spiritual ruse my family played in the Christian patriarchy movement, my natural hair was long and covered by a white handkerchief. Cutting it was a disgrace. A disgrace, I tell you. That's what Biblical Paul said 2,000 years ago in 1 Corinthians 11.

Like most everything I grew up with in this male-dominated subculture, hair was a symbol. It was a sign of subordination to my authority figure – my father and God. Perhaps as a consolation bonus, it was also my glory. That's what Paul said. That's what my authority figures dictated.

There wasn't much to do with my hair. My sisters, mom and I washed it, brushed it, pulled it back into a barrette or ponytail holder and covered it with our head coverings. The white pieces of cloth we used to cover it was a symbol – white for purity and my dad saw them as a deference to him; we wore them to show our allegiance to God. Again, it was mostly Paul's idea.

Sometimes we French braided it. A few of us had bangs; some women at church curled theirs. One wife raved about how her husband brought home a curling iron and hairspray. I listened to her talk about how she'd wanted the items for a long time and a tiny seed was planted in my young heart: I wanted the ability to buy my own curling iron and hairspray if I wanted to.

It was about more than just a curling iron and hairspray.
I wanted to choose for myself.
I wanted to taste liberation.
I wanted freedom.

When I was 19, my mom, siblings and I disconnected ourselves from the Christian patriarchy belief structure. We started doing heathenistic things like wearing jeans and, yes, cutting our hair.

Though it was no longer a symbol of modesty or religiosity, my hair represented me – a symbol of wild will and sometimes-unkempt behavior. A nervous twirl, a sassy flip, a careless bun, a pensive filter, my hair kept me safe. I could hide behind it. My "fat" face felt less puffy and my round cheeks were minimized when my hair surrounded it.

By choice, I kept it long for 10 years and I used the length as a barometer of religious affiliation. If it got too long, I would ask my friends, "Do I look like a Baptist?" Sometimes they would answer, "Yeah, it's borderline Mormon." And I would go have three or four inches cut off.

Most typically, I threw it on top of my head in some conglomeration of a messy bun just to get it out of my way. I joked that one day I might cut it all off.

In June 2013, one of my best friends was diagnosed with an inoperable brain tumor. I remember sitting at my desk hearing the news for the first time thinking, "If she loses her hair, I want to lose mine." It was something I could DO in a situation in which I felt so powerless.

Strangely we had connected over hair throughout the course of our friendship. She had long hair; I had long hair. Two months before the seizure that would lead to her diagnosis, we were in Haiti together. We were sweating at a community dining room table after a day of volunteering at a local hospital and she said, "Do you want me to French braid your hair?" I told her I didn't know how to French braid hair and she said, "I'll teach you."

Two months later, the seizure. The cancer diagnosis. The radiation treatments. She started waking up to find chunks of hair on her pillow. The shower drain became filled with pieces of it.

Three months after her diagnosis, it was Sept. 2, my 30th birthday. I sat in a stylist's chair and asked her to cut off my nearly 13 inches of hair and style what was left into a pixie cut.

It was a safe middle ground between the memories of my dad and pastors telling me that long hair was modest, mandated, spiritual, and society that told me hair is beauty; beauty is hair. I was scared to let it all go.

But then, in a moment, I wasn't.

It was an evening – the one when my cancer-fighting friend was sitting in a chair surrounded by her closest friends. There was music playing and most of us were singing along while one by one we took hold of the electric razor and shaved off a portion of her remaining hair. The locks fell gracefully and gathered at her feet. It felt both unjust and beautiful. Everyone was crying – her tears fell the largest – then we were laughing, then closing eyes and raising voices.

Three of her friends arrived that night with shaved heads, motivated by my supposed courage to cut my hair. I was inspired by their bravery to go all the way.

I called one of them into the bathroom – the one who had brought the razor – and I asked her if she would shave my head.

"Do you want a No. 2 or No. 3 razor?" she asked. I chose No. 2.

She began to shave and the previous pixie disappeared.

She finished and I looked in the mirror at the person looking back at me. Same eyes. Same round cheeks. Same forehead wrinkles. I rubbed my hand quizzically over my shaved scalp, then both hands slowly as if I was handling a prized artifact for the first time.

My hair and my head. What had once been a symbol of subordination became an overflow of loyalty and a meager offering of sacrificial friendship. It was a small gesture of assurance, the way a friend might silently reach over to clutch your hand in a darkened theater, or just before the roller coaster plummets. You are not alone. I am here too.

In the way that the darkest nights bring the most spectacular of mornings, this was the ultimate transference of authority – from the dogmatic interpretations of ancient Scriptures, from society's dictation of beauty, from my own insecurities and into the hands of my True Self.

This was beauty. This was power. This was I, liberated.

Holly Wise is a lecturer at Texas State University where she teaches multimedia journalism, editing for clear communication and the beginning and advanced levels of news writing. She is an accomplished newspaper and web journalist, and has worked for several Texas newspapers, including the Austin American-Statesman.

She recently completed her memoir, "And Then This Happened," which documents her journey from being raised in a seclusive branch of the Christian Patriarchy movement to who she is today.

She is the founder and executive director of VoiceBox Media – a news service that specializes in solutions journalism. She has traveled to Kenya, Haiti and Ethiopia to cover social entrepreneurs and changemakers. Last summer, she developed an internship program and now works with teams of journalists and public relations practitioners who are committed to honing their solutions skillsets. She has taken teams of students to cover national and global stories, such as the Baltimore activists and community hospitals in Nicaragua.

CHAPTER 8

A HAIR STORY, FROM PLAITS TO LOCS

by Linda Lockhart

Thinking back over a lifetime, my earliest recollection of hassles with hair goes back to the mid-1950s, when I was about 4 years old. My mother went to work early, and my father, who went to work in the afternoon, was responsible for getting me up and out. He would feed me and help me get dressed before taking me out on errands or just for fun.

He could do a lot, but the one thing Daddy didn't do was comb my hair. As I think back on it today, it's possible that my hair didn't need to be combed every day. But on one particular morning, it did. So Dad hustled me over to the next-door neighbor, a nice lady with little girls of her own, and asked her to work her magic on me.

After sitting between Miss Lumilla's knees for the requisite amount of time, I was released with a head-full of neatly spaced, tiny plaits — a not-uncommon do for little girls in my neighborhood.

Back at home, Daddy thought a bit of color would be nice, so he added little barrettes to nearly each plait. I was content, and off we went. All was well, until Momma got home. She was not happy.

"You look like a little pickaninny," she said.

I didn't know what a "pickaninny" was, but from the tone of Momma's voice, I knew I didn't want to look like one. I think that's the first time I ever felt bad about my hair.

Over the next few years, as my hair grew longer (and thicker), began the biweekly pilgrimage to The Hairdresser. Usually with my mother, and sometimes with my grandmother, I made these regular trips to a beauty shop, sometimes in my neighborhood, but other times across town.

At first, there was the routine shampoo and dry, followed by that dreaded "press" with the "hot comb," where The Hairdresser would use a heavy, metal comb, heated in a special stove, to straighten out my tightly clinched "naps."

With this mission accomplished, The Hairdresser — and through the week my mother — would style my hair into three neatly positioned braids — two at the back and one at the side. Today, I'm not sure why we opted for that asymmetric style. But back in the day, it worked just fine.

This arrangement would usually look nice for about two weeks — unless my hair got wet — for any reason. That's when the hair would "revert" to its natural state.

Over the next few years, I progressed from braids to the "press-and-curl," still using the hot comb for the initial straightening, but adding the "curling iron" to lay down neat rows of loopy curls that were then combed through into a lovely arrangement. At night I would wrap lengths of hair around "curlers" or "rollers" and tie them down tight with a scarf.

Then came the high school years and the "permanent relaxer." This chemically altered state was an answer to this girl's prayers. Now I could swim, or sweat or get caught in rainstorm with no ill affects.

By college in the 1970s, "Black and Proud" was all the rage. I bravely joined the "Movement," by letting my hair "grow out." No more chemicals for me. I sported an afro that would have made activist-scholar Angela Davis proud. It was big, round and perfectly shaped.

Styles over the next decades included corn rows, Jheri curls, Wave Nouveau, and short natural, finally bringing me to my current minimal-maintenance choice of dreadlocks.

Today, I have a hairstyle that is true to my heritage. It is free of chemicals. I thank entertainer Whoopi Goldberg and writers Alice Walker and Toni Morrison for showing me the way.

My hair makes me happy.

Linda Lockhart is a child of God, wife, mother, grandmother, journalist and lover of good times. She works at St. Louis Public Radio and stopped stressing about hair years ago.

CHAPTER 9

'WHITE CHOCOLATE'

by Elizabeth Ann Atkins

D on't hate me because I love my hair.
For too long, I loved other people's hair, and loathed that the natural texture of my own made me different.

But now I am truly a Hair Goddess because I praise God for blessing me with unique hair that I love.

Let me count the ways ...

First, it's super low maintenance. A few times a week, I wash it, comb out tangles, apply a little mousse, and let it air dry.

Other days, I run wet fingers through it a few times, and boom, the curls come back to life. Other days, inspire clipping it up in a twist, or pulling it up in a ponytail, and voilà. Done.

Aside from a quick trim every few months, and a weekly coconut oil treatment, that's it.

Second, it has a different personality every day. At the moment, thanks to a sweaty, windy bike ride, it's a sunburst of small corkscrew curls dancing around my shoulders. Other days, it's more wavy and appears longer.

Third, it changes colors with the seasons. Right now, a lot of time in the summer sun turned it bright yellow. By February, my hair will be a honey-butter swirl.

Fourth, and most importantly, it represents my unique white chocolate blend of African American, Italian, French, English and Cherokee. And it is a crowning glory that celebrates my parents' courage to love across America's often vicious racial divide.

They did this, even though the bishop damned them to hell because my father was a Roman Catholic priest who left the church to marry a much younger black woman. Even though their lives were threatened and they hid out with me and a rifle in a hotel room during the 1967 riots.

Because they dared to defy America's racial and religious conventions, people were cruel to them, just like people have been mean to me.

"You look like you stuck your finger in a light socket!" boys taunted in elementary school. "Your hair is so frizzy!"

I would cringe with shame. And when I looked in the mirror, I wished I could be like my girlfriends, who were all sporting the hottest hairdo in America: the Farrah Fawcett. Their fine, straight hair was "feathered" back in perfect layers around their faces, and they carried little combs in the back pockets of their designer jeans (which I didn't have, either), to whip out and flauntaciously fluff their feathers. (Yes, I made up a word, I'm a writer).

Meanwhile, I restrained my giant yellow hairsplosion in a braid or a bun.

Then as a teenager, I experimented with products that defined the mass into distinct corkscrew curls, and I began wearing it down.
"I love your curly hair," girls and women praised. "I spend so much money on perms to curl my hair!"

Finally I began to love my hair.

So when I said, don't hate me because I love my hair, it's not about being arrogant.

It's about being grateful for what God blessed me with as a symbol of the human harmony that my parents' union epitomizes.

My opening statement is also about a woman who is happy with who she is, how she feels, and how she looks.

Too many of us, regardless of race, either truly hate ourselves or are afraid to love and celebrate ourselves for fear of being accused of thinking we're "all that" or that we're "full of ourselves."

So I say, proudly proclaim what you love about yourself, whether it's your hair or something else.

Because our kids are watching. Our daughters, of course, but our sons, as well.

When my son — whose dad is African American — turned 13, he proudly wore a big afro, an anomaly (and source of fascination) amongst his mostly white classmates. I couldn't have been more proud of him for never experiencing the I-wish-I-had-Caucasian-hair phase that I had at his age.

Instead, he was proud and bold, empowered by flaunting his best and most authentic self to the world.

As we all should, and wearing our God-given crowns with pride and love.

"I'm like sweet, white chocolate fondue in the American melting pot — unique, but bitter? I'm not," declares **Elizabeth Ann Atkins** in her autobiographical poem, *White Chocolate*, also the name of her first novel.

The African American, Italian, French, English and Cherokee TV show host is the best-selling author of 17 books, an actress in two films, a screenwriter, an award-winning journalist and an inspiring speaker. With a master's degree in Journalism from Columbia University and a bachelor's degree in English Literature from the University of Michigan, the fitness enthusiast was a guest on *Oprah* after losing 100 pounds. Visit ElizabethAnnAtkins444.com.

NATURAL WOMEN

by Valerie Rollins Vaughn

Photographer Valerie Rollins-Vaughn uses her camera and her connections to help other girls redefine their own standards of beauty. www.project unlabeled.com

CHAPTER 10

EMBRACING MY HAIR AND HEALTH

by Paula McDade

Growing up as a little brown girl, I spent a great deal of my time wishing I had long flowing hair. My hair was dense, but fine in texture and easily tangled.

The beauty standard that was presented to me was the same one that every other black girl was shown in magazines, on television and in the media – straight and tame with as much length as possible. My favorite playtime activity would involve the use of a towel or a sweater draped over my head like hair as I would swing it from side to side like I imagined other long haired beauties would.

I felt powerful with this new pretend hair, like I was the ultimate beauty queen. My mother wasn't the type of hair-combing mom who enjoyed dealing with my thick mane, and at the age of nine or ten I started learning to comb it myself.

At about age eleven, my mother started sending me to the beauty shop to have my hair hot-combed. I hated every minute of that process from the detangling and combing to the actual heated metal iron Miz Doris used to run through my hair as the hot grease sizzled on my scalp. I would usually end up getting burned because I flinched and squirmed during the agonizing process. This would continue all through my adolescence until I turned sixteen.

As a teen I became very skilled at styling my own hair and even learned to cut it myself in the popular styles other girls my age were wearing. One day, I was at my boyfriend's house when his sister and her friends were sitting around putting a white creamy substance on their hair. I was fascinated at the process because I'd never seen anything like it. They explained to me that they were "relaxing" their hair and the chemicals they were using would give them a smooth, straight look. I always admired the hairstyles they wore, and they convinced me to try it.

One application of creamy crack and I was hooked! I finally discovered a way to get away from the hot pressing comb with less burning, detangling and agony. Once I tried relaxing my hair, I never went back to pressing again. I would save, scrimp and borrow to be sure I had enough money to keep up my new hair routine at least once every couple of months. I learned how to apply the relaxer myself, making it even more convenient because I didn't have to wait for someone to be available to apply it for me. This way of dealing with my hair became my new "norm."

I had always taken great pride in my hair, arranging my life, schedule and activities around managing my hair. On rainy, windy or humid days, I dreaded having to figure out how I was going to protect my style from certain destruction. On "good hair" days, I felt like I was on top of the world, and on bad hair days, my world would crumble.

The irony of this whole story is that somewhere deep down in my core, I always wanted beautiful, curly hair. I longed to wear a big curly afro and let my hair really do what it was created to do. The only thing holding me back was the unknown. I didn't know how people would react. I didn't know if men would find me attractive with the style, so I kept my desires to myself and continued to straighten, but all of that would come to a halt in May 2009.

One day I started to feel like something was very wrong in my body. I was experiencing chills, weight loss, lack of appetite and nausea. I made an appointment to see my doctor and he ran a series of tests. The following day he called me at work and I stepped out to take the call.

The diagnosis was autoimmune hepatitis, a disease where my immune system was rapidly destroying my liver. Although the prognosis was not fatal, it was serious and I needed immediate treatment. My doctor immediately prescribed a strong dose of steroids to arrest my immune process and stop the damage.

During the course of treatment over the next few months, I gained fifty pounds, developed severe acne and my hair was rapidly falling out. I was devastated, confused and afraid of what was happening to my body. The medication that was meant to help me was actually destroying me. My hair was not only shedding, but breaking all around the edges and it was now baby fine and fragile. I could no longer relax my hair because it was not strong enough to withstand the chemicals and the structure of my strands was very different. I was back at square one and needed to learn my hair all over again.

I began to seek the help of a naturopathic doctor to help me wean off of the strong medication I was taking and find natural alternatives to my healing. During that time I also made the decision to "big chop" my hair to get rid of all the relaxed hair. Although I was very unsure about what I was doing, I knew I had to do something because my current styling techniques weren't working.

After taking the plunge, I was filled with uncertainty because I felt as if I looked like a boy with no hair.

It didn't take long for me to find alternative ways to accessorize my hair to make myself look more feminine. About three months into that first natural hair journey, I cheated and put a texturizer on my short hair to create some waves.

In 2011, I made the decision to permanently transition to natural by doing one more big chop and I haven't turned back. It took a health crisis to force me to deal with my hair, but I'm glad it happened.

Hair is more than an accessory you wear on your head, it is your essence and your personality. Your hair is as unique as your fingerprints, with its own likes and dislikes. It will respond to the right treatment and products if you take the time to nurture your hair.

Our hair can help us identify hidden health issues and nutritional deficiencies in our diet. I now embrace and love my natural hair, but I don't look down on others who choose a different method of styling.

We are all individuals and as women of color we have many choices on how to style our hair. Choose the best for you and keep your real hair as healthy as possible.

Keep in mind that hair eventually does grow back if you make a major decision you regret, and just have fun with it!

Paula McDade can best be defined as a multitalented creative.

A gifted graphic designer, McDade is the CEO of Stellar Creative, a boutique firm specializing in creative strategies for small businesses, individuals and companies to help represent their brands with excellence. She is a dynamic inspirational speaker on topics relevant to women in the areas of healing from trauma and abuse. Last year, she became the founder and creator of Captured and Crowned, a ministry for women and girls whose lives have been affected by trauma and/or abuse.

She has written the Captured and Crowned devotional and journal, which is currently featured on the YouVersion bible app. Youversion currently has more than 700 different translations, in over 400 languages reaching an international audience across all continents. She is also a co-author in an amazon best seller entitled "igniting the fire: a woman's guide to setting ablaze in ministry, business and life."

CHAPTER 11

IT WAS A CROWN

by Kamara Jones

When I want to do something I'm scared to do, I tell a lot of people I'm going to do it. Then that way once I've told enough people the pressure from them — *When are you going to go natural?* — will outweigh my fear of doing whatever I'm scared to do.

That's exactly what I did when I got closer to deciding that I was going to go natural. I hadn't had a relaxer in so long it almost felt like a missed opportunity to get all of my new growth relaxed again.

People suggested that I "transition" by cutting off my relaxed hair as my natural hair grew in. But I am too impatient for that. Other people suggested I "transition" by wearing a weave after cutting off my relaxed hair. But I am too real for that. If I was going to go natural, I wanted people to see my natural hair. I also didn't want to replace one expensive hair process — relaxer — with another — weave.

These suggestions weren't wrong, they were just wrong *for me*. If I was going to go natural, I was going to do a "big chop" — cut all of my relaxed hair off down to the new growth.

People have different reasons for going natural and I had several but the primary one was this: I needed to come to terms with my natural hair, and my body and beauty in relation to it. Also, twenty more years of relaxers didn't seem sustainable to me and I was tired of the time and money associated with the relaxer process. And every time I went back I felt more and more like I was on a conveyor belt waiting to be turned into a widget.

When I told one of my childhood friends my reasons for going natural she said, "For you this is more of a cleansing process."

I couldn't have said it better myself. I wasn't doing it to be or feel more black. I feel and am pretty black. I wasn't doing it because I thought relaxers were evil. I have nothing against relaxers. (In fact, I can't say at this moment that I'll never get another one again.) I just wanted to go for a run after work without having a two-hour process to get my hair back the way it was.

So one day I just walked into a barbershop. I had planned to call and schedule an appointment but every time I tried I got nervous and hung up the phone. The barbershop was everything I thought it would be. Checkered floors, barbicide, the best of black music playing on the stereo... It even had its own version of the *Barbershop* movie characters Eddie and Checker Fred.

And it brought back memories, too. When I was a little girl my dad used to take me with him to get his hair cut and afterwards we'd get a chocolate shake.

His barber was an elderly man who seemed to me like a king among men. Steady hands and conversation. ... I was so nervous about the cut that when the barber asked me what I wanted a jumble of nonsense rolled out.

"I h a v e a r e l a x e r b u t I ' v e b e e n g r o w i n g i t o u t f o r t w o m o n t h s a n d I t h i n k I h a v e e n o u g h n e w g r o w t h t o c u t t h e r e s t o f i t o f f b u t l e t m e k n o w i f I d o n ' t b e c a u s e I d o n ' t w a n t t o l o o k l i k e h i m."

I proceeded to point to a man getting his hair cut who was all but bald.

"OK," he said smiling. "We'll see what we can do. Fortunately, for you, I don't have another client after this."

That made me scared. I was pretty much locked into cutting all my hair off at this point.

When I got in the chair I showed him a picture of Chrisette Michele's hair right after she decided to go natural.

"Yeah, you have enough new growth to do that," he said.

He immediately started cutting. I thought I'd feel sad but I didn't. There's nothing more annoying than having two textures of hair, and getting rid of one of them gave me a sense of relief.

And the fact that I wouldn't have to flat iron it every day gave me a sense of relief too.

When he started cutting the hair on the back of my neck he asked me to bend my head down. When he returned cutting the hair on the sides and the top of my head, my head was still bent down.

"Hold your head high," he said. "Be proud."

I had honestly just forgotten to hold my head back up, but what he said in hindsight was profound.

My natural hair wasn't a dunce cap — oh no, it was the exact opposite. It was a crown.

Kamara Jones is the press secretary for a federal agency. She lives and works in Washington, D.C. She is originally from a small town in Missouri.

CHAPTER 12

HAIR APPARENT?

by Amy Raymond

I should love my hair.

Not to gloat, but most people would be happy to have hair like mine. It's thick, grows quickly and has the kind of curls many women say they want.

I won't say that I hate it. It just doesn't feel like it's mine.

I feel like a follicle fraud.

When I picture myself, I see straight hair, because for the first 22 years of my life, that's what I had.

Straight, rather thin hair that tangled easily. Not the typical hair you expect for a Latina.

And, unlike most women, I liked it. I never wanted curly hair. It's too soft. Too feminine. It's cute.

"Cute" is the one thing I never wanted to be.

I wanted to be a force of nature. Unflappable. Unstoppable.

Mother Nature had a different idea, the witch.

In college, I grew my hair to my waist. It started getting noticeably thicker and the texture was changing, but it was still straight. I didn't give the change much thought.

I graduated from college and entered the professional world as a reporter.

I had a young face, and the waist-length hair didn't help. It was time for a drastic change.

Amy, right, her sister, left, and her grandmother and cousin.

Hello curls.

My hair didn't spring into ringlets upon being cut to my shoulders, but it was a big difference.

What started as wavy ended up outright curly.

My great journey to accept me for me was being sent down a curlicue path.

For a few years, I straightened the curls. I've since just given in. The coarser and kinkier my hair gets, the more difficult it gets to overcome nature's forces.

People who know me as an adult are surprised by pictures of me as a little girl.

People I grew up with and have reconnected with on social media ask if I started perming my hair.

Some people say, "It's just hair." But we all know it's not that simple.

Getting to the root of the change isn't easy for me — and it may be the reason I have spent far too much time thinking about my hair, and not just accepting the change.

I'm adopted. My parents are white, and I have a sister, Ange, who is also adopted, and Latina, but not my biological sibling.

My sister and I didn't look like the other members of our family — and I have never thought we look that much alike.

I am one of a kind, and, even as a little girl, I was OK with that.

My mother told me recently of a trip to New Mexico we took when I was very little. My sister marveled that the people in the mall all looked like her and me. In other words, they were Latino. My sister saw the difference, too.

I don't know her inner dialogue about how she looks. She's more private about such things.

I never felt I missed out on anything by being adopted. I've always been grateful for how my life turned out.

I did wonder sometimes what it would be like to have other people around who looked like me. I think I ended up deciding that I would rather be unique.

I have always liked myself and didn't understand when I was little why the rest of the world didn't see how awesome I really am.

I was never the skinny one. I was always lighter skinned than my sister, but I didn't want to "pass" and not acknowledge my Hispanic heritage, as some suggested I should.

I grew up in a house that didn't focus on appearance or weight, for which I am eternally grateful. My parents encouraged my sister and me to engage with our Latino heritage as much as we chose. My mom made a point of buying dolls for us that had dark hair or darker skin, so we had images of beauty that looked more like ourselves.

I see now how advanced that thinking was for the early 1980s.

Despite the love and support my sister and I both got at home, plenty of others made note of the fact that I was "the big one" compared to my sister.

As far as I was concerned, if someone didn't like me because I wasn't a size 0, they were revealing that they weren't worth my time or energy.

And, despite growing up in the era of perms, I liked my hair and rebuffed any effort to curl it.

That stubborn streak served me pretty well for a long time. I think it's much healthier to accept what makes me beautiful rather than trying to make myself acceptably beautiful by anyone else's standards.

And it's the reason when I picture myself, I have straight hair. It's not the hair of anyone's dreams, but my own.

Nor am I a size 0 in my mind's eye. And that's cool, too.

Maybe someday I'll straighten my hair in a more permanent way.

Maybe someday, when I close my eyes, I'll see a girl with curly hair, but is still tough and not too cute.

At least when I close my eyes now, I still see this very important thing: someone who is unique and who is awesome.

Amy Raymond is the Senior News Editor and works in the Presentation Desk, which handles copy editing, headline writing and design for all Oklahoman sections, except Sports, as well as Web duties. She has worked at The Oklahoman since graduating from Oklahoma Christian University in 1997 with a degree in biology. She has handled various duties at The Oklahoman, including staff writer, Newsroom 101 coordinator, and Viva Oklahoma editor.

CHAPTER 13

HAIRSCAPES

By Clytie Bunyan

Growing up in a home where I was the youngest of four sisters, there was a lot of hair envy, mainly coming from me. I've always wished I had hair like my sisters Suzanne and Arona — coarse, thick hair that stays in place when styled. Hair that looks like Oprah's.

Instead, mine is thin, fine kinky hair, the kind that requires setting spray to hold up through the day; the kind that has no body but just hangs flat.

When I was a child, everyone loved to comb my hair. It was easy to braid, rarely tangled or knotted up. My mother or sisters would braid my hair, accessorize it with ribbons or decorative clips and I'd be off to school, church or wherever a family or social event led.

But my experiment with hairstyles, what l call my hairscapes, began when I left my parents' house and moved to the United States, where I discovered I could do whatever I wanted with my hair -- except I couldn't.

First came the Jheri curl years, the curly look that gave the illusion of full-body hair. It was a good look for me but required way too much moisture products. I don't like sleeping with anything on

67

Clytie, right, and her sisters.

my head so my pillows were changed often.

Then came the years of my longest experimentation — the relaxer years. I've known some good hair stylists but those first years with relaxed hair, when my sister Linda and I were each other's hairdresser, were the best my hair ever looked. I've always credited sponge rollers for that. Even wind-blown, I could rake my fingers through my hair and it would mostly fall back in place.

I began seeing professional stylists after college, but usually after a week I'd end up pulling my hair back into a ponytail look. For years, that became my signature look, and still is my fallback style. It's classic and simple and, with makeup and appropriate jewelry, my ponytail is dramatically knockout.

In my quest to achieve the Oprah look, or at least the full-bodied look like my sisters' hair, I decided to try a weave. I was diligent about seeing the stylist every week or every other week so she could make adjustments and make sure my hair had good conditioning. After about a year, I decided to take a break from the weave and wear my natural hair.

I was standing at the kitchen sink the day I took the weave out when my husband walked in and yelled, "What the hell have you done to your hair?" I asked what was he talking about; all I did was take out the weave. "You're practically bald on the top of your head," he said.

He was right. Yes, I'd felt the pull when my stylist would make adjustments to the weave but I trusted she knew what she was doing. She never told me I was losing hair. Not once. I was angry and highly disappointed but I let that go to focus on how I would look in public. I certainly had no intention of walking around with visible bald spots. I have a highly-visible position at work so it's important to me that I look neat and professional always. My hair is a big part of that look. So I turned to wigs. I've been wearing them ever since, and along the way found a stylist who painstakingly worked to regrow hair I thought was gone forever.

I'm very particular about what type of wig I wear. It has to look like a natural fit, one that doesn't scream "wig" to the casual or curious observer. But under the wigs is natural hair that I can wear as that classic ponytail.

My healthy hair today is courtesy of two Tobys: Tobbie, the stylist I leaned on in desperation when I discovered my post-weave hair loss, and Toby, my current stylist, recommended by a coworker, who looked at my hair and said, "Um, um, um. Girl, you can either relax it or color it, but you can't do both."

Well, at 54 and greying, I chose color, and it's been surprisingly wonderful wearing natural, colored hair.

That is, when I'm not wearing a wig.

Clytie Bunyan joined The Oklahoman in 1989 as a Metro desk reporter. She later moved to the Business desk to cover real estate and presided over extensive coverage in the 1990s about the then-uncertain future of the Skirvin Hotel. She also has covered small business and the retail beats. She was named assistant business editor in 2000 and business editor in 2003.

She now oversees the Business and Lifestyles sections of The Oklahoman, and manages four traditional beats: Health, Common and Higher Education and City Hall.

Bunyan also heads up Community Engagement and Staff Development for the News and Information Center at The Oklahoman.

CHAPTER 14

THE COURAGE TO BECOME YOURSELF

by Sonya Walker

ebster defines courage as mental or moral strength to venture, persevere, and withstand danger, fear, or difficulty, the strength to support unpopular causes;

Wow, what a definition!

It clearly tells us the characteristics that we must have in order to have courage. It will take having a mind to persevere and withstand those around you who choose not to support, encourage, or inspire you to be yourself or fulfill your God-given dreams.

This is what I would like to call becoming yourself in the midst of adversity. It means to become yourself when it's not popular, and not praised, to take the risk of becoming an individual instead of conforming to their idea of whom you should or should not be.

I remember when I finished high school and I tried to go to a university because my friends were going but I had a strong desire to become a hairstylist and makeup artist. When I decided to take the path or course that God had for me to fulfill the passion that was weighing on my heart, my friends and family talked about me and said many things that could have stopped me but I was determined.

When I told them my plans I wasn't asking them for permission, I was making a declaration that this is who I am and this is who I want to be.

I didn't ask anyone to go with me and I didn't ask anyone to pay for it and neither to co-sign for it. I have learned over the years that when you tell people who you are and what you are going to do, somehow they think that you are asking for their permission and their help.

I am very passionate about having the courage to become yourself simply because I know what it is like not to have support, to be criticized, and to become discouraged because the ones who you thought would want you to become yourself are those closest to you. When in reality those are the ones who do not believe in you.

I know what it is like for God to open up doors for you and to find yourself standing by yourself because you thought when you got to this place in your life the people whom you love would be standing there cheering you on, instead of stepping on your hopes and dreams.

What do you do when the people you love or care about try to shatter the dreams or ideas of you becoming yourself? I tell you what you do: "take another step."

I remember speaking at a Women's Conference a few years ago and the message that God gave me was, "The Agony of Defeat." In this message I told them that you have to continue to walk toward your destiny even while you are in pain. To walk toward your dreams even when you feel like fainting. To run toward God even when they tell you that you are not going to make it and having done all to stand, stand therefore. To smile even when you feel like crying because it will take everything you have to become the person you desire to be.

No one is going to favor you when you are trying to become yourself; instead many will oppose you. I don't want any of you to be fooled into thinking that things are easy for me because I fight adversity all the time.

Not knowing who is for you and then learning that the ones closest to you are trying to destroy you. I don't want you to be fooled into thinking that fulfilling your dreams is going to be easy.

Don't fool yourself into thinking that everyone is going to jump on your bandwagon, and send you flowers because you decided to write your book, go back to school, open your business, or climb the ladder of success! If it was that easy then you wouldn't need courage.

In the Bible whenever God would call someone to walk into or to fulfill their destiny He would say this:

"Be strong and of good courage; only be thou strong and very courageous."
Joshua 1:6, 7

God continues to encourage them to be strong and to have courage and that He is with them.

Well that is good news because if God be for you and He is for you then you can conquer anything. I was walking through my house the other day and a scripture and topic came to mind. This is the scripture:

"And when Paul had gathered a bundle of sticks, and laid them on the fire, there came a viper out of the heat, and fastened on his hand. And he shook off the snake into the fire, and felt no harm."
Acts 28:3-5

In this I heard the Holy Spirit say, "sometimes it takes fire to find out who the snakes are in your life." When you decide that you are going to get the courage to become yourself then that is when the people whom you thought was for you, you learn are against you. We must be like Paul and shake them off.

When you read that scripture in its entirety you will see that the same people who criticized him turned around and praised him. You can't be moved either way; I want to encourage you to take another step toward becoming yourself.

I will close with this: when I decided to open up a boutique it was ok as long as I was online but when I decided to open up a physical location I had adversity but I was determined and today the same people who was against me now try to act like they are for me because of its success. But, guess what?

I am not moved either way, I just continue to take another step. What if I had listened to the critics who are on the side line complaining I wouldn't be here talking to you today. Be strong. Be encouraged. Be empowered. Become yourself for the best is yet to come.

Sonya Walker is an image/fashion consultant, transformational life coach, and an ordained minister — a woman full of purpose who is very passionate about empowering women to love themselves. Sonya has been in the beauty industry for 20-plus years as a hair, makeup, and fashion stylist. Sonya was called into ministry in 1995 and has since ministered to countless numbers of women.

"I have always loved the complete image from head to toe. I have had clients who were beautiful outwardly, yet their inner beauty was completely opposite. When God gave me the vision to open Essance Salon, I found myself ministering to women one by one. I then realized that God had more in store for me and that my purpose was more than just hair, makeup, and fashion."

Sonya began receiving invitations to come and speak at Women's Conferences on beautifying women from the inside out through the word of God. After she ministered, the women would come back with their heels, makeup, and dressed up. "God was changing their perception of themselves through His word."

CHAPTER 15

'FRO FRISKING, SECURITY & THE POLITICS OF HAIR

by Yvette Walker

The Transportation Security Administration announced in April 2015 that it no longer will pat down 'natural' hair.

When I say 'natural hair,' I mean black women's hair that is not chemically relaxed, as that appears to be where most of the ire has centered.

I'm talking, afros, dreadlocks, curly twists, "sister locs" and big, frizzy curls.

I haven't flown since I've gone natural, and that's probably a good thing. I would NOT appreciate a TSA officer's gloved hands (which has touched any number of other unsavory things) going through my hair.

My hair in its natural state: curly and free.

However, I wear my hair both curly or straight, depending on my mood. My straight hair (achieved through blow-drying, not chemicals) is TSA-acceptable. My curly hair, not so much.

Celebrity Solange Knowles, sister of Beyonce, and known for her keen fashion taste and her super-natural hair, said on Twitter: "Discrim-FRO-nation. My hair is not a storage drawer…"

Right on, Solange. I am NOT carrying (anything), TSA officers.

Two women, Malaika Singleton and Novella Coleman, filed complaints with the TSA and their voice was heard. Coleman, it has been reported, is a staff lawyer with the American Civil Liberties Union. In a letter responding to the women, the TSA said it would offer training and would track further patdown complaints.

The complaints generated a lot of press coverage about the policy. Shortly after, the TSA sent a statement out to media outlets:

"TSA reached an informal agreement with the ACLU to enhance officer training. Racial profiling is not tolerated by TSA. Not only is racial profiling prohibited under DHS and agency policy, but it is also an ineffective security tactic."

Thanks to Malaika and Novella for ending the madness.

But it's not the end of natural hair discussions, because as more black women embrace relaxer-free hair, the more society will take note.

Danielle C. Belton wrote for the website The Root about styling her natural hair, and told readers that it's not easy having this kind of hair. She writes that her hair can be difficult to style into society-friendly looks, is time-consuming, and is not the romanticized kind of hair that is "wash and go."

"My hair — while strong, long and my dominant feature — is a carefully crafted myth that can easily be shattered by stuff like "the wind," "water" or "the scarf fell off while I was asleep."

—Danielle C. Belton

It appears Ms. Belton and I have similar kind of hair. My main reason for going natural is that relaxers and color are two chemical processes, and my hair only wanted one. After brittle and breaking hair made this clear to me, I opted to cut out the relaxer. NOT the color. (Are you kidding? I'm gracefully aging, but aging all he same.)

Add to this the creation of "natural hair wigs" and natural hair weaves, and women feel pressured to make their curly hair look like something that is not natural at all. Wigs are made to be perfect, where every hair stays in place. Natural hair is just the opposite. Sometimes I want to scream, "stop comparing my hair to that wig!"

Or, as Ms. Belton wrote, "That afro is a lie."

It might seem hard to believe, but I'm not complaining. I love my hair. It's just another feature that sometimes is used to define me.

Despite the TSA change, I heard the unfortunate news this summer that some friends had witnessed 'fro frisking at airports. The TSA stands by its rule change, but apparently some guards haven't gotten the new orders.

Watch your 'fros, people! Everyone else is.

CHAPTER 16

GABBY DOUGLAS IS MORE THAN HER HAIR

by Yvette Walker

Originally published in 2012, after the Summer Olympics, on NewsOK.com

G abby Douglas is a gold medalist and Olympian at 16 years of age.

That's more than any troll on Twitter can say for herself.

In fiction, a troll is a hideous, wicked creature lacking humanity. In the real world, they post unkind tweets about other people. The definition fits the people who decided to criticize American gymnast Gabby Douglas for having what they describe as unkempt, sweaty hair during the women's gymnastics competitions at the Olympics in London.

Never mind the girl was working as hard as her body would let her. Never mind she was twisting and contorting on the uneven bars, the floor exercise and her nemesis, the balance beam. Never mind she was perspiring, as any human will do when putting your body through such a workout.

And, sadly, many of those trolls appeared to be African American women. Sad, but not surprising. This is not a racist tweet trend. It's an example of black women digitally beating up a little girl whose star is rising.

Were they trying to be funny? And if so, why focus on her hair? Any black woman can answer that. It's the old war of "good hair" vs. "bad hair."

Among some African Americans, "good hair" is straight or slightly wavy, similar to the kind of hair on the heads of Caucasian people. "Bad hair" is tightly curled, kinky, or "nappy," and is the kind of hair found on the heads of many people of African descent.

The debate has gone on for years in the black community, but digital technology is making it easier to air this dirty laundry.

One of the first to report the Olympic hair hate was the online magazine SportyAfros.com, which was picked up by Jezebel.com and others. Monisha Randolph, a regular contributor to Sporty Afros, examined three of the main complaints found on Twitter:

"She needs some gel and a brush …"

"Someone needs to give her a hair intervention …"

"She has to "represent" …"

Stunned, Randolph wrote, " … the last time I checked when you play a sport, you sweat. I know I do. And when a Black woman who has chosen to wear her hair straight begins to sweat, her hair will (not might) begin to revert back to its natural coily, curly or kinky state. Does Gabby need to stop every five minutes to check her hair? No."

"Hair Goddess" author Linda Jones, who does not straighten her hair (see Chapter 3), is reclaiming the idea of "bad hair" and turning it into a positive. Jones is a journalist and the founder of A

Nappy Hair Affair, which organizes grassroots hair grooming sessions that are known as Hair Days. She also is author of "Nappyisms: Affirmations for Nappy-Headed People and Wannabes!" Thursday morning Jones posted on Facebook: "I don't care if she was wearing a Mr. T Mohawk, Gabby represented for us all."

In a private Facebook conversation Thursday night, Jones told me her group's message goes deeper than hair. "It is to promote positive images of people of African descent. Gabby, our young role model, does that hands down.

"Whoever made those disparaging remarks about Gabby's hair while she was going for the gold, has bought pettiness to a new low. It smacks of jealousy to me — and also idleness."

At first, I was afraid that Douglas' brilliant performance at the Olympics might become just another chapter in the tired, old story about black women's hair.

But social media trends are brief, and backlash against the trolls soon took over. Thursday, as Douglas soared and jumped and tumbled and strutted to her gold, there were few criticisms of her hair to be found on Twitter. In fact, some of the original "haters" seemed to change their tune.

After Douglas won the individual all-around gold, an interviewer asked her what it all meant to her. She credited God, her family and endurance.

"Hard days ... that's where champions are made," she said.

Exactly, Gabby — in the gym, not in the hair salon.

ADDENDUM

ANOTHER HAIR REVUE

by Yvette Walker

Book Review: "Me, My Hair and I," edited by Elizabeth Benedict (Algonquin Paperbacks, 316 pages)

"Hair Goddess" joins the ranks of another excellent compilation of essays about hair. This excerpt originally was published September 2015 on NewsOK.com

My mother had a trademark saying about how women had to go through a lot to be acceptable in society's view and in societal standards.

I hadn't thought about that saying in a while — "You have to suffer to be beautiful." A new compilation of essays about hair, beauty and standards titled "Me, My Hair and I" brought it rushing back.

Edited by author Elizabeth Benedict, the amusing, entertaining and sometimes poignant book features 27 authors writing about the obsession that is women's hair: the texture of it, the length of it, the lack of it, the color of it and even where it appears on their bodies.

Are there really enough hair stories for 27 women to write about? Well, let's see ... hair-ironing, chemotherapy as a stylist, African-American hair, sibling hair rivalry, thick hair, thin hair, hair that makes you look old, hair and cultural traditions, wigs, braids, dreadlocks ... this list goes on.

• There was the woman who always wanted long, luscious locks — ever since her mother cut her hair for convenience sake. Rebecca Newberger Goldstein writes that "my mother was tired by the time my sister and I were born."

• Jane Smiley writes about her hairstyle, called "Femme Fatale. Or maybe it was Harlot. The bonus I got with this haircut was that I could put a hat on, take it off and have the hair fly out to its intended shape again. It was just like Barbie in every way."

• And there were identity issues deeply rooted (no pun intended).

For black women, wearing hair in its most natural state is a common sight today. Companies — mom-and-pop and mainstream — sell products to women with coarse, curly hair.

The writer I most identified with was Marita Golden and her tales of hair-straightening in the kitchen at her mother's hot comb-wielding hands. In the 1960s and '70s, the hot comb was a torture device that loving mothers heated on the stove burner and applied to their daughters' liberally greased hair.

Golden writes of this pursuit of "white girl hair" and the disappointment when those silky straight tresses "went back," meaning reverted to their natural, hated state.

The hot comb still exists, but for many reasons (including chemical straightening and the preponderance of natural hairstyles) it is not used as much as in decades past.

Indeed, like many other women of different ethnicities, I have left behind the chemical jar and let my natural curls and coils fly free.

Still another essay gets to the heart of the matter. Elizabeth Searle, whose mother must have known mine in another life, took the words out of my mouth.

She writes, "It was worth all the hard brushing and twisting needed to create ponytailed perfection. I was learning this lesson young: beauty hurts."

Ah Elizabeth, I feel your pain.

MORE TITLES

If you are interested in reading more about women, hair, race and culture here is a partial list of good examples:

Another book, **Hair Story**, a historical look at African and African-American hair, has been revised and updated in paperback. It is published by St. Martin's Griffin books and is written by authors Ayana D. Byrd and Lori L.Tharps, with a foreword by MSNBC host Melissa Harris-Perry. Other releases:

Hair Raising: Beauty, Culture, and African American Women by Noliwe M. Rooks

Going Natural; How to Fall in Love with Nappy Hair (Going Natural How to Fall in Love with Nappy Hair Book 1) by Drs. Mireille Liong-A-Kong

Hair Matters: Beauty, Power, and Black Women's Consciousness by Ingrid Banks

Stylin': African American Expressive Culture, from Its Beginnings to the Zoot Suit by Shane White and Graham White

Naked: Black Women Bare All About Their Skin, Hair, Hips, Lips, and Other Parts by Ayana Byrd and Akiba Solomon

From the Kitchen to the Parlor: Language and Becoming in African American Women's Hair Care by Lanita Jacobs-Huey

The Politics of Black Women's Hair by Althea Prince

Rapunzel's Daughters: What Women's Hair Tells Us About Women's Lives by Rose Weitz

Pageants, Parlors, and Pretty Women: Race and Beauty in the Twentieth-Century South by Blain Roberts

ABOUT THE AUTHOR AND EDITOR

Yvette Walker has a passion for women's culture: the politics of hair, fashion and standards of beauty. She wears her hair both curly and straightened without chemicals, but doesn't castigate any woman who chooses to wear her hair differently.

A Chicago native, she has witnessed the "mainstreaming" of black natural hairstyles in the workplace – from braids to dreadlocks to non-chemical styles worn free.

Walker is an award-winning newspaper and website editor. After graduating from Northwestern University's Medill School of Journalism, she has worked for newspapers in Gary, Ind.; Austin, Texas, Dallas, Detroit, Kansas City, Mo., and Oklahoma City.

She started down this natural hair journey in 2013 after years of devotion to the "creamy crack," and believes she has experienced growth — both personal and through the length of her hair. She was a speaker at the 2015 Oklahoma Naturals Expo in Oklahoma City.

FAQ

Frequently asked questions on natural hair

By Yvette Walker

Why do women go natural?

From my observations, most African American women jump into the natural hair experience out of fear, fun or frustration: fear of damage done to hair after years of using chemicals; fun, for a change of pace; frustration of the amount of time and money needed to consistently maintain relaxed hair. No matter which, most don't have the information they need at the start of their natural hair journey.

Do you have to cut off most of your hair and start over?

Some women decide to do the "big chop" and cut off most of their hair. Frequently, it can be a convenient way to start the natural process. But it is not a requirement. I decided not to do a big chop. Instead, my stylist trimmed my damaged ends, braided my hair into a flat beehive, and sewed in a weave. I wore this for 3 months, and when I took it out, she trimmed the remaining permed ends off. This worked well for me, but you must choose your own path.

Can you wear natural styles in the workplace?

Of course! It does depend on the culture of your office, how formal the attire is and what your bosses prefer. But any woman with natural hair can find a style that is acceptable and appealing in her workplace.

Does wearing your hair natural vs. chemically straightened

affect your self-esteem?

It should not, but our cultural standards can affect one's opinions of one's looks. Decades of society telling women to look one way vs. another can beat you down. However, I defer to writer Sonya Walker on this. She writes in an earlier chapter:

> "No one is going to favor you when you are trying to become yourself; instead many will oppose you. I don't want any of you to be fooled into thinking that things are easy for me because I fight adversity all the time.
>
> "Not knowing who is for you and then learning that the ones closest to you are trying to destroy you. I don't want you to be fooled into thinking that fulfilling your dreams is going to be easy.
>
> Don't fool yourself into thinking that everyone is going to jump on your bandwagon, and send you flowers because you decided to write your book, go back to school, open your business, or climb the ladder of success! If it was that easy then you wouldn't need courage."

You've made the decision, what's the next step?

Find a stylist who is concerned about the HEALTH of your hair, not just the style. There are many naturalists across the country and the world. Ask trusted friends and colleagues. Once you find one, write down all the questions you have and have a conversation with that person. Don't be afraid to look for someone else if you don't like what you are hearing, or you don't like the surroundings that person works in.

What products should you use?

There are myriad products on the market these days, from major manufacturers to home-grown products. Again, ask your stylist and people you trust.

Is the decision different for women than for men?

Our writer, Mashaun D. Simon, made a decision purely for his career (see Chapter 6). Others are influenced by family, and, as I mentioned earlier, fear or frustration about the state of their hair. There is no one factor.

Do people with naturally kinky or curly hair suffer more intolerance than women with straightened hair?

It depends. Simon did at his internship. You must judge your office dress policies and wear your hair accordingly – in a neat natural style. If you work in a highly creative environment, adjust your styles to match. Have fun!

Does wearing your hair natural imply you are more "black" than others with straightened hair?

Absolutely not. Says our writer Alison Bethel McKenzie:

> "I go to the hairdresser every week without fail. I deep condition and straighten and, on occasion, flat iron. While I don't frown on the "Happy to Be Nappy Movement," I also embrace choice. Straight. Curly. Wavy. Permed. Locked. Twists. Wigs. And, kinda – weave.
> "I am no less black, or pro-black because I choose straightened hair."

What is a Dark and Lovely?

Someone who playfully refers to the popular commercial relaxer used today. Says McKenzie:

> "I am a woman who is proud of being so-called

"dark and lovely," a spin on the permanent hair straightening process that I use so regularly."

Can non-African Americans suffer hair intolerance, too?

Certainly. Writer Amy Raymond, who is Latina, recalls others criticizing her curly hair:

> "My great journey to accept me for me was being sent down a curlicue path.
>
> "For a few years, I straightened the curls. I've since just given in. The coarser and kinkier my hair gets, the more difficult it gets to overcome nature's forces. ...
>
> "I have always liked myself and didn't understand when I was little why the rest of the world didn't see how awesome I really am."

Why is hair so important? Why is it a point of contention?

That is a question that will continue to be debated through the ages. Hair and standards of beauty have evolved but take root in society.

Ayana D. Byrd and Lori L. Tharps, the authors of "Hair Story – Untangling the Roots of Black Hair in America" refer to hair's value throughout centuries. Some even believe in hair's spiritual qualities:

> "Wolof tradition says that women had the power to make men crazy for them by calling on the power of the genies in the hair. ... Because a person's spirit supposedly nestled in the hair, the hairdresser always held a special place in community life."

We see this today, don't we? And don't you know women who cut their hair if they feel they have "bad energy"? I certainly do.

INDEX

NOTES

NOTES